Fieke Tissink

THE REMBRANDT HOUSE MUSEUM AMSTERDAM

Ludion

FOREWORD

Not long ago the Rembrandt House Museum underwent a veritable meta-morphosis. Since it was opened to the public in 1911, Rembrandt's old home had essentially functioned as a gallery in which Rembrandt's prints were exhibited – now, however, it gives visitors a far more intimate picture of the setting in which one of the world's greatest artists lived and worked. The radical restoration and subsequent reconstruction were made possible by the construction of a new wing, which was opened in 1998 and now houses the permanent exhibition of Rembrandt's prints.

The reconstruction of the interior was preceded by in-depth scientific and historical research. The inventory of Rembrandt's property drawn up after his bankruptcy in 1656, which accurately records every item, room by room, together with drawings that Rembrandt made of parts of the interior, formed the basis for the work. These and other sources provided the team of experts who drew up the reconstruction plans and supervised the work with the indispensable points of reference they needed to design a histori-cally sound reconstruction of the whole interior.

The reconstruction of the Rembrandt House is founded on the convic-tion that, in an age when the sense of history seems to be disappearing in large parts of society, historic monuments are an evocative way of keeping our ties with the past alive. The Rembrandt House believes that bringing the past to life in this historically truthful manner contributes to maintain-ing and enhancing an awareness of history and knowledge of the roots of European culture.

This change in the concept of the museum, which now focuses both on the prints and on Rembrandt's house, meant that it was time for a new museum guide. We are grateful to the publishers, Uitgeverij Ludion, for enabling us to produce this new version. I would like to extend my warmest thanks to everyone who has contributed to the production of the guide. I hope that this little book will help foster a better understanding and greater appreciation of Rembrandt, his house and his art.

Ed de Heer
Director

Contents

Self-portrait with Saskia 1636, etching

The Life of Rembrandt van Rijn

Leiden

1606	Rembrandt is born in Leiden on 15 July. He is the ninth child of the miller Harmen Gerritszoon van Rijn and Neeltgen Willemsdochter Zuytbrouck.
c. 1613-1620	Rembrandt attends the Latin School.
1620	Rembrandt is enrolled at the University of Leiden.
1622	Rembrandt goes as an apprentice to the Leiden painter Jacob van Swanenburch. He stays for three years.
1625	For more than six months Rembrandt studies with the history painter Pieter Lastman (1583-1633) in Amsterdam.
	Back in Leiden, Rembrandt sets up as an independent artist.
	Rembrandt paints his earliest dated work, *The Stoning of St Stephen* (Lyon).
1628	Rembrandt takes his first pupil, the fourteen-year-old Gerrit Dou.
	Constantijn Huygens, secretary to stadholder Frederick Henry, visits Rembrandt and his friend Jan Lievens in Leiden. He compares their work, regards them both as geniuses and praises Rembrandt, in particular, to the skies. Some time later Rembrandt receives commissions from the stadholder's court in The Hague through Huygens.
1630	Rembrandt's father dies in Leiden.
1631	Rembrandt lends the considerable sum of one thousand guilders to the Amsterdam art dealer Hendrick Uylenburgh.

Amsterdam

	At the end of 1631 or soon afterwards, Rembrandt goes to Amsterdam where he lodges with Uylenburgh. The art dealer has a sort of workshop, which Rembrandt probably runs.
1632	Rembrandt paints his first group portrait, *The Anatomy Lesson of Dr Nicolaes Tulp* (Mauritshuis, The Hague).
1634	On 22 June Rembrandt marries Saskia van Uylenburgh, his employer's niece. The couple continue to lodge with Uylenburgh for almost two years.
c. 1635	Rembrandt gets one pupil after another, among them Ferdinand Bol, Govert Flinck and Gerbrand van den Eeckhout.
	Rembrandt rents a house in the Nieuwe Doelenstraat.
1637	Rembrandt moves to a house called 'De suijckerbackerij' on the Binnen-Amstel.
	Rembrandt acquires a great many prints, drawings, art albums and curiosa at auctions.
1639	Rembrandt buys a prestigious merchant's house in the Breestraat, the present Rembrandt House. It costs 13,000 guilders. He has to take out a large mortgage.
	Rembrandt receives the commission to paint *The Night Watch*.

1641	Titus is born. He is Rembrandt and Saskia's fourth child and the only one to survive to adulthood.
1642	Saskia dies.
	Geertje Dircx enters the household to look after the infant Titus. Rembrandt and Geertje embark on a relationship.
	In this year Rembrandt completes his masterpiece *The Night Watch* (Rijksmuseum, Amsterdam).
1647	Hendrickje Stoffels moves in as Rembrandt's housekeeper.
1649	Problems with Geertje Dircx result in an action for breach of promise against Rembrandt. The painter has to pay alimony of two hundred guilders a year.
	Hendrickje has supplanted Geertje in Rembrandt's affections.
1650	Rembrandt has Geertje Dircx committed to the house of correction in Gouda.
1653	Rembrandt receives a huge bill for arrears of payments for the purchase of his house.
	Rebuilding work is done on the house next door, causing Rembrandt considerable nuisance.
	Rembrandt paints his famous *Aristotle Contemplating the Bust of Homer* (Metropolitan Museum, New York).
1654	The birth of Cornelia, the illegitimate daughter of Rembrandt and Hendrickje.
	Rembrandt paints the portrait of Jan Six (Six Collection, Amsterdam).
1656	On 14 July Rembrandt petitions the High Court of Holland for *cessio bonorum*. This means that he surrenders all he owns to be sold for the benefit of his creditors. He attributes his financial problems to 'losses suffered in trade and also damages and losses at sea'. The bankruptcy is handled by the Amsterdam Insolvency Office.
	On 25 and 26 July an inventory of Rembrandt's possessions is compiled. It includes the exceptional art collection.
1657 and 1658	Rembrandt's property is sold at auction. On 1 February 1658 the house in the Breestraat is auctioned.
	In May 1658 Rembrandt, Hendrickje, Titus and Cornelia move to a rented house on the Rozengracht (now number 184).
1659	Rembrandt authorizes his son to act for him.
1660	Hendrickje and Titus become the owners of Rembrandt's art dealing business. Rembrandt formally works for them and continues to paint.
1662	Rembrandt paints *The Syndics of the Cloth Makers' Guild* (Rijksmuseum, Amsterdam).

Isaac and Rebecca, known as 'The Jewish Bride' *c.*1665, Rijksmuseum Amsterdam

1663	Hendrickje Stoffels dies.
1667	The Italian Grand Duke Cosimo de' Medici visits Rembrandt and describes him as a famous artist.
1668	Titus marries and dies in the same year, not yet 27 years old.
1669	Rembrandt becomes a grandfather: Titia is born, six months after the death of her father Titus.
	Rembrandt paints three more self-portraits in the last year of his life.
	Rembrandt dies on 4 October at the age of 63. He is buried in an anonymous rented grave in the Westerkerk.

Rembrandt in Amsterdam

At the end of 1631 Rembrandt van Rijn (1606-1669) moved from Leiden, his birthplace, to Amsterdam. The largest and most prosperous city in the United Provinces was not unfamiliar territory to the ambitious young artist. He had already received commissions to make portraits of wealthy Amsterdam citizens and he had sold his work there, but it was not until 1631 that he made his home in the city. Amsterdam acted as a magnet for anyone who wanted to earn money, and was extremely important in cultural terms: for artists, the city was rich in opportunity. Rembrandt found lodgings with the art dealer Hendrick Uylenburgh on the corner of the Breestraat and the Zwanenburgwal. There was a workshop incorporated in Uylenburgh's successful business, where young artists were trained. Rembrandt became a teacher there, and painted predominantly portraits. Within a remarkably short space of time, the Leiden-born painter established himself among the respected artists and craftsmen in Amsterdam.

1639 was an important year for Rembrandt. It was in this year that he received the prestigious commission to paint a portrait of members of one of Amsterdam's militia companies. This painting was subsequently to become world famous as *The Night Watch*. He bought the house in the Breestraat (now the Jodenbreestraat) – the present day Rembrandt House – in the same year. By then, Rembrandt was already a celebrated artist.

The Company of Captain Frans Banning Cocq and Lieutenant Willem van Ruytenburch, known as 'The Night Watch' 1642, Rijksmuseum Amsterdam

At the end of the 16th century Amsterdam underwent a period of unparalleled growth as a result, among other things, of an influx of immigrants from the Southern Netherlands. The number of inhabitants rose from 65,000 in 1580 to 120,000 in 1631. The city had to be extended. A large new district grew up on the eastern side, with Sint Anthoniesbreestraat as the main thoroughfare. In 1601 the present lock, the Anthoniessluis, was built on the site of the medieval defences, and this made further expansion possible. Sint Anthoniesbreestraat was continued as far as the present-day Jonas Daniël Meijerplein. The new district was to be a select neighbourhood composed mainly of merchant's houses. To ensure that it remained so, it was decreed that artisans who used hammer, anvil and fire were not allowed to set up in business here.

Detail of the map by Balthasar Floriszn (1625) showing the house of Hendrick Uylenburgh and the Rembrandt House

Hans van der Voort of Antwerp had two houses built in this new neighbourhood, one of which was later to be the Rembrandt House. He moved into the corner house with his brother, the painter Cornelis van der Voort, and sold the house next door. The new owner was Pieter Belten. In 1608 he and his family moved into the house where Rembrandt was later to live. Belten was a well-to-do merchant, who used part of the house to store his wares: indigo, cloves, ginger and peppercorns.

When Pieter Belten died in 1626, his two children inherited the house. They both married in the following year and moved into the house with their partners. However, the house was too small for two families and it was remodelled and extended. Jacob van Campen – the architect who went on to design the Town Hall in Dam Square – was responsible for the work. He added another storey to the front part of the house, eliminating the original step gable. The present gable dates from this period. It is a triangular pediment with a cornice in the Dutch Classicist style, which was quite progressive at this time. The second important alteration was the building of a four-storey extension behind the side room, which made the courtyard considerably smaller. Despite all the work they had had done on it, the families did not live in this house for very long. The last member of the family moved out in 1633. It was not until 1639 that Rembrandt bought the house. Part of it had been let in the intervening years.

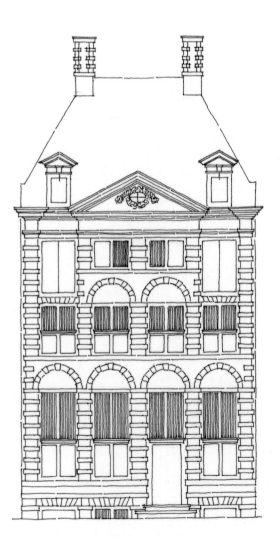

Work had meanwhile started on building the first part of the ring of canals in Amsterdam. The wealthy people moved to this new area and the prices of the houses in the older districts fell. The neighbourhood around the Sint Anthonies-breestraat was no exception and it was here that Portuguese Jewish immigrants – and artists like Rembrandt – settled. The purchase contract was drawn up for him in 1639: the house cost 13,000 guilders. A very substantial sum compared with the annual wage of a labourer at the time, which amounted to a couple of hundred guilders at most.

Rembrandt was able to pay for his house in instalments. When he moved into the house, his neighbour on the left was the merchant Salvador Rodrigues. Until 1645, the portrait painter Nicolas Eliasz Pickenoy lived in the house on the corner on the right, the former house of the art dealer Hendrick Uylenburgh, with whom Rembrandt had lived between 1631 and 1635. Diagonally opposite Rembrandt lived the writer, printer and rabbi Menasseh ben Israel.

The front of the house after the renovation by Jacob van Campen (drawing: H.J. Zantkuyl)

Rembrandt lived in the house in the Breestraat for almost twenty years. Many of his masterpieces were painted in this period, among them *The Night Watch,* which dates from 1642. Rembrandt lived in this house with his wife, Saskia. She was born in Leeuwarden in 1612, and was Hendrick Uylenburgh's niece. Rembrandt probably met her in her uncle's house. They were betrothed in 1633 and married in 1634. She brought with her a dowry of more than 40,000 guilders, a vast fortune at the time. Their first child, Rumbartus, was born at the end of 1635, but lived for just a few months. Only their fourth child, Titus, was to survive infancy.

After Saskia's premature death in 1642, Rembrandt employed Geertje Dircx, a childless widow from Edam, to look after Titus. She became Rembrandt's mistress. Their relationship ran into trouble in 1649, probably as a result of the arrival of the much younger maid, Hendrickje Stoffels, who had come to work in Rembrandt's house two years earlier. The difficulties with Geertje Dircx culminated in an action for breach of promise as a result of which Rembrandt was ordered to pay alimony because he had allegedly promised to marry Geertje.

After her departure, Geertje's place as housekeeper and lover was assumed by Hendrickje. She became Rembrandt's support and helpmeet. Despite this, they never married. The explanation for this can be found in Saskia's will, which stipulated that if Rembrandt remarried he would have to pay her family half of the estate she had inherited. This would have involved a sum in excess of 20,000 guilders – an amount Rembrandt could never have hoped to raise, given his financial position. In 1654 an illegitimate daughter, Cornelia, was born to Rembrandt and Hendrickje.

Meanwhile Rembrandt had built up a flourishing artist's workshop, with numerous pupils and assistants. His studio tended to attract artists who had learned their trade elsewhere and wanted to learn to work in Rembrandt's style – a style that was extremely popular. As 'apprentices' they contributed to the workshop's output. Following his early training in Leeuwarden, Govert Flinck (1615-1660) moved to Amsterdam to work in Rembrandt's studio as an assistant to the master and to improve his professional skills. Ferdinand Bol (1616-1680) worked with Rembrandt until about 1642, and then set up on his own. Gerbrandt van den Eeckhout (1621-1674) also studied with Rembrandt, as did Samuel van Hoogstraten (1627-1678), Carel Fabritius (1622-1654) and Nicolaas Maes (1634-1693): all artists who themselves went on to become famous painters after their apprenticeships with Rembrandt.

Rembrandt had great success with his paintings and prints. He also made good money from teaching his pupils. He could certainly afford the hefty sum of 13,000 guilders that his house cost in 1639. Nevertheless, in 1658 he was forced to sell his house. His financial difficulties stemmed from a number of causes.

For several years after he finished *The Night Watch,* his artistic output was much lower than it had been before. He stopped painting portraits, a significant source of income. He also lived in great style. He amassed a collection of art and curiosities on which he must have spent a fortune. And it is by no means impossible that Rembrandt, like many other people at the time of the naval wars with England, had made injudicious investments. In any event, his financial problems did not, as is sometimes asserted, have anything to do with a decline in interest in his work.

Over the years, the house had meanwhile dropped in value because the district had become less sought-after. The building also had structural defects. It was built on marshy land, and soil compaction had caused considerable subsidence.

In 1658 Rembrandt finally moved to a rented house on the Rozengracht, where he remained until his death. His house was sold for 11,218 guilders.

*Self-portrait in painter's garment c.*1652, drawing, The Rembrandt House Museum
A drawing shows us how Rembrandt dressed when he was working – in a long coat fastened with a cord around the waist. Below the drawing, a later 17th-century hand has written 'drawn by Rembrandt van Rhijn after himself as he was dressed in his studio'.

In 1661 the house was jacked up to prevent further subsidence, and divided into two separate dwellings. In the 19th century the house was further split up and enlarged by the addition of two storeys on the rear extension. In 1906 the painter Jozef Israëls suggested that the Rembrandt House should be restored and turned into a museum in honour of the world-famous artist.

The Rembrandt House before the restauration by K.P.C. de Bazel

1906 saw widespread celebrations to mark the 300th anniversary of Rembrandt's birth. A plan to turn Rembrandt's house into a museum to mark the occasion was mooted. At that time the house belonged to the Spits brothers, who ran a shop selling watches and haberdashery.

The plan – the initiative of the painter Jozef Israëls – was well received. The City of Amsterdam bought the building for 35,000 guilders and in 1907 transferred the title to the house to the newly founded Rembrandt House Trust. The trustees' aim was to return the house 'to the state in which it may be deemed to have been when it was lived in by the painter Rembrandt van Rijn'. This ambition proved controversial from the outset and a fierce debate ensued. Jan Veth (1864-1946), a painter, art critic and member of the Board of Trustees, was a particularly fierce opponent of the idea. He believed that 'Rembrandt should be allowed to speak for himself', and argued that the house should become a gallery in which Rembrandt's etchings could be exhibited. Veth also took control in the debate about which architect should be appointed, and in February 1908 K.P.C. de Bazel (1869-1923) was commissioned to undertake the restoration.

De Bazel restored the facade and reinstated the original layout of the house. However, he decided against a reconstruction of the 17th-century interior. Instead he deliberately opted for a layout that made the house a suitable place to exhibit prints and drawings. The historic house thus acquired a contemporary interior, which by no means pleased all those concerned. It did not, after all, convey any sense of what the house had been like when Rembrandt lived and worked there three centuries before. The Board of Trustees were unable to agree among themselves on the principles of restoration. Shortly before the opening the controversy reached such a pitch that Jan Veth stepped down as a Trustee. Nevertheless the museum was officially opened on 10 June 1911 in the presence of Queen Wilhelmina. The reactions were predominantly positive.

Loans, gifts and purchases rapidly swelled the print collection. The museum now has 250 of the 290 etchings by Rembrandt, in various states. Not all the prints can be kept on permanent exhibition. Works on paper cannot tolerate too much exposure to light. However, the rotating exhibitions mean that there are always etchings by Rembrandt on display.

Although the Rembrandt House did not provide a glimpse of the painter's 17th-century home, it became a popular museum, attracting many visitors from all over the world. The growing numbers of visitors made it essential to expand the museum. A great deal of hard work finally paid off in 1998, when the new wing was opened. The etchings were transferred to the new building, leaving the way open to restore the Rembrandt House to its original 17th-century state. A team of experts, led by the historian of architecture Henk Zantkuyl, made the plans for the restauration. At last it was possible to achieve what the founders of the museum had had in mind at the beginning of the 20th century: to give an impression of Rembrandt's house as it must have been during his lifetime.

The new wing of the Rembrandt House was opened on 7 May 1998. A hypermodern façade gleams next to the 17th-century artist's home. The architects, Zwarts and Jansma, deliberately sought the contrast. The façade appears to have been made out of a huge etching plate, which is divided into horizontal strips. An enlarged detail of Rembrandt's etching *Abraham's Sacrifice* has been engraved into the copper. The façade is largely windowless, because the etchings that are exhibited inside cannot tolerate daylight. And yet the overall impression is not shut-in because there are glass doors in the entrance and the offices on the top floor have large windows.

On every floor of the new wing, visitors have a view of the old house and the little courtyard. Large glass walls make it easy for people to see exactly where they are. The interior of the new wing was designed by Peter Sas. The visit begins in the new wing, and visitors enter the old house through the basement. At the top of the house the tour continues in the new wing, going through the galleries, where there are often special exhibitions, and back down again. Visitors look first at Rembrandt's house and studio and then at his work.

Reconstruction: back to Rembrandt's day

When Rembrandt bought his house in 1639, he paid only a small fraction of the purchase price. He was supposed to pay back the remainder in instalments, but he preferred to spend his money on his collection of art and curiosities (see page 53).

In 1656 Rembrandt was unable to compound with his creditors any longer: in June a petition for his bankruptcy was filed. A list was compiled by an official of the Insolvency Office, who made a meticulous record, room by room, of the furniture, paintings, household goods, prints, drawings, statues, weapons and rare objects he found. This inventory proved an invaluable guide in the restoration of Rembrandt's house in 1998 and 1999, listing as it did precisely which objects were to be found in which rooms, and thus revealing what the different rooms were used for. 17th-century objects were borrowed, acquired as donations and bought for the reconstruction. New furniture was also made in the 17th-century style using the techniques of the time. The result is a faithful reconstruction, which has restored Rembrandt's house to him.

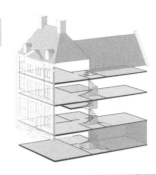

The house is on four storeys, linked by a wooden spiral staircase. The floors are deal, glazed tile, stone and marble. The ceiling beams are painted red and ochre, the walls are plastered and whitewashed. The skirtings and mantelpieces are decorated with 17th-century Delft blue and polychrome tiles. The interior has been restored to the period around 1650.

The tour begins in the kitchen in the basement.

This kitchen was the centre of activity in the house. The fire was usually kept burning. The water pump was in here, and this is where the household cooked and ate. The maid slept in the box bed.

The small door beside the hearth opened on to an alley that led to the Zwanenburgwal. The door by the sink opened on to the courtyard. The privy was here, above a cesspit. All sorts of objects used by Rembrandt's household were found in the cesspit during the renovation of the house in 1997.

There was probably also a covered gallery in the courtyard. Wooden lean-tos like this were not uncommon in the yards of 17th-century houses. All sorts of household chores were done there. Sheltered from wind and weather, the maid, the woman of the house and the man of all work could take advantage of the daylight for as long as possible.

There are indications that Rembrandt raised the height of the gallery before 1643. It is possible that he did this in order to paint *The Night Watch* under it. At more than three metres by four and a half, this huge portrait of a local militia company would not have fitted into Rembrandt's studio, so it may well have been painted under the lean-to. When it was finished, it would probably have been rolled up and carried out of the house to the Kloveniersdoelen – the headquarters of the company that had commissioned it. This world-famous work now hangs in the Rijksmuseum in Amsterdam.

Kitchen utensils

Regrettably, the 1656 inventory does not tell us much about what was in the kitchen. 'A pewter water pot, some pots and pans, a small table, a cupboard, some old chairs, 2 cushions', that is all. This meagre list of kitchen equipment might indicate that Rembrandt was allowed to keep the majority of his pots and pans.

Life in the kitchen
Was it here that Geertje Dircx and Rembrandt quarrelled about a financial arrangement? With the arrival of Hendrickje Stoffels, Geertje became redundant both as a maid and as Rembrandt's mistress.

Rembrandt's Cesspit

Fragments of an earthenware pot with two ears

Dutch majolica dish

The cesspit to Rembrandt's house was in the courtyard outside the kitchen. Before the sewers were laid, every house had one of these pits, where the contents of the privy ended up and the kitchen waste was disposed of.

This pit was discovered during the restoration work on the Rembrandt House and work started on emptying it in the autumn of 1996. A painstaking excavation of numerous later layers of muck and broken crockery revealed the stratum of 17th-century finds. From it emerged a great many shards and objects, including an almost perfect jug, an Italian dish and a Majolica plate. There were also two *grapen* – a sort of cooking pot with three feet. Both pots had a strange white coating inside. Further research revealed that one of the pots had contained a mixture of chalk and size, and the other white lead. They must have belonged to Rembrandt and were evidently used by him in his studio. He probably put his dirty brushes in pots like these while he was working. The pot containing remnants of chalk and

Glass cup: fragments of such a cup were found near the Rembrandt House

Stoneware jug from Westerwald

size was undoubtedly used to prepare the ground for his canvases and panels.

The majority of the finds were ceramics – shards of pots, plates and dishes. Glass was also recovered, a pewter spoon, a wooden lace bobbin, a wooden butter pat and some toys.

These toys were made around the middle of the 17th century, so Rembrandt's children, Titus and Cornelia, may very well have played with them. Among the finds were a miniature milk jug and some marbles made from fired and glazed clay. Small, apparently not very valuable everyday objects like these certainly bring the life of Rembrandt and his family a little closer.

THE ENTRANCE HALL
(Voorhuys)

This elegant, spacious hall was the first room that visitors saw when they entered Rembrandt's house. It was obviously the residence of a well-to-do citizen. Costly materials like marble were used to create an air of distinction. The walls were covered from top to bottom in paintings by Rembrandt himself and by his pupils. This was the entrance to Rembrandt's art shop. The customers could take a seat on the chairs ranged around the walls.

The inventory describes them as 'four Spanish chairs with leather, two ditto chairs with black seats, a deal wood dais'. The latter referred to the small platform by the window. Anyone sitting on the chair placed here would have a good view of what was happening in the street, and would also be out of the cold draughts. Daises like this one were quite common in the 17th century and they were sometimes shown in paintings of the period.

A mother and child are standing on a checked tile floor. Through the open doors we get a view of the cellar, the entrance room and the street outside. In the entrance room we see a chair on a wood dais.

A mother and child in a cellar room c. 1660, Pieter de Hooch, Rijksmuseum Amsterdam

On the wall hangs *The Lamentation for Abel* by Rembrandt's teacher Pieter Lastman (1583-1633).

Adam and Eve mourn their son Abel, who was killed by his brother Cain. The story of the lamentation is not found in the Bible but in apocryphal writings: commentaries on the Bible.

Rembrandt managed his affairs and kept his papers in the tiny room by the stairs.

Rembrandt had his shop, his art dealing business, in the anteroom, the side room at the front of the house. This is where he received his clients, who were invited to take a seat on one of the 'seven Spanish chairs with green velvet seats'. Rembrandt probably served his clients a glass of chilled wine, since the inventory lists a marble cooler. Glass in hand, seated on the elegant chairs, potential buyers could feast their eyes – the walls were covered with dozens of paintings by Rem-brandt himself and by his pupils. He also dealt in paintings by other masters. We know, for example, that he had works by Flemish and Italian artists. The nucleus of his collection, however, consisted of 17th-century Dutch paintings. On the day that the inventory was compiled, 25 July 1656, the paintings in this room included 'a prospect by Lucas van Leyden, a tronie by Rembrandt, a ditto by Brouwer, a woodland scene by Hercules Seghers, a Tobias by Lastman'.

Marble

The floor and the columns either side of the fireplace are marble. The mantelpiece, however, is made of marbled wood, which was very fashionable in the mid 17th century. This skilled work was much cheaper than real marble and yet looked exactly like it. Often the only way to tell the real from the imitation is to place a hand on the marble: real marble is always cool to the touch.

The present box bed was not in this house originally; it comes from a 17th-century house in Culemborg. There was however a similar, finely carved bedstead in this room, intended for overnight guests.

To the left of the mantel hangs a painting by Rembrandt's pupil Ferdinand Bol (1616-1680).

It is a copy of a work by Rembrandt, *Christ Appearing to Mary Magdalene* (1638).

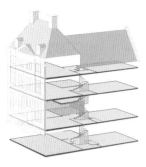

Rembrandt was not only a great painter – he was also a gifted draughtsman and a pioneering etcher. He probably printed from many etching plates in this room. The inventory tells us that there was an oak printing press in here.

The fine 17th-century tiled floor was laid during the recent restoration work. The tiles originally did duty as ballast in a barge that sank in the Zuyder Zee in the 18th century. The vessel was recovered when one of the IJsselmeer polders was drained.

Interior of a printer's studio 1642,
Abraham Bosse, etching

Etching technique
Rembrandt was a true master of the
technique of etching. An etching is
an impression on paper pulled from
a copper plate. The plate is coated
with a mixture of asphalt, resin and
wax. Known as the etching ground,
this coating is resistant to acid. A
scene or design is drawn into the
coating using an etching needle. The
copper is exposed where the needle
goes through the etching ground.

The plate is then submerged in a
bath containing an acid solution.
The acid bites out – etches – the
exposed lines of the drawing, creat-
ing grooves in the plate. The etching
ground is then removed and the
clean plate is inked with an ink-pad

or a roller. The surface of the plate is
then wiped clean; the ink remains
in the grooves.

At this stage a dampened piece
of paper is laid on the copper plate.
The plate and the paper are passed
between the rollers of the press. The
paper absorbs the ink from the
grooves and the design appears in
reverse on the paper. The damp
sheet is hung up on the line to dry
like so much washing.

The Salon *(Sael)*

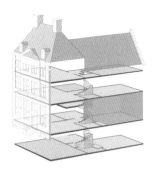

This was Rembrandt's living room and the room where he slept. Rooms of this period often had several functions – in this case living and sleeping. In the 17th century the Salon was the finest room in the house. It is a high-ceilinged room housing numerous paintings, among them works by his teacher Pieter Lastman.

A drawing by Rembrandt shows us what the room looked like in his day: his wife Saskia is lying in bed. Rembrandt married her in 1634 and she appears in many of his drawings and paintings. They had four children, only the last of whom, Titus, survived infancy. After Titus's birth, Saskia increasingly had to keep to her bed; she was sickly and weak. In the drawing the maid keeps her company. Saskia died in 1642; she was only thirty.

Saskia in bed c. 1642, drawing, Fondation Custodia, Paris
This drawing was an important source of information in the reconstruction of this room.

Pieter Lastman (1583–1633)
Rembrandt's teacher

Rembrandt learned his trade as a history painter with Pieter Lastman in Amsterdam some time around 1625. Lastman lived in the Breestraat – the street where Rembrandt himself would later live.

Lastman was considered to be one of the leading history painters of his day. He had an innovative approach to depicting stories, concerned as he was with the emotions of his protagonists, with their expressions and gestures.

A great deal was expected of a painter of 'histories' – exemplary stories taken from the Bible, classical antiquity and mythology. He had to be a master of all sorts of specialisms, from landscapes and interiors to people, animals and inanimate objects. He also had to know all the rules of composition, of perspective and of appropriate costume. In 17th-century art theory, the history painter was rated most highly – above the portrait painter, the still life specialist and the landscape artist.

Pieter Lastman was an important history painter in his own time. The Danish king, for instance, commissioned three biblical scenes from him. His fame was later to diminish and he became known almost solely as the man who taught Rembrandt and Jan Lievens.

At the beginning of his career Rembrandt's choice of subjects and the way in which he constructed his compositions was very reminiscent of his teacher's work. His paintings, like Lastman's, were colourful and crowded with figures in action. There are several paintings by Lastman in the Salon of the Rembrandt House, including *Christ on the Cross,* dating from 1616. A crowd has gathered at Golgotha where Christ hangs on the cross between two criminals. Lastman portrayed Jesus's mother and Mary Magdalene weeping at the foot of the cross, the soldiers casting lots for Christ's garments and a motley collection of onlookers.

Rembrandt owned a large collection of drawings in red chalk by Pieter Lastman.

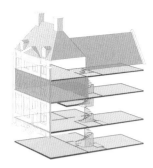

This is where it all happened: between 1639 and 1658 Rembrandt painted many of his masterpieces in this large room. The room smelled of linseed oil and turpentine, and in the winter of the peat that was burned in the two cast-iron stoves. The stoves were needed to keep Rembrandt and his models (often nude) warm, as well as to dry the paint.

The room faces north, ideal for a studio. The light enters evenly through the windows; Rembrandt was able to control and temper it to some extent by closing the shutters over the bottom windows and adjusting the white cloth over one of them.

On the shelves around the walls are objects that Rembrandt and his pupils used as props when they were painting: armour, helmets, cuirasses and weapons of all kinds, plaster casts of classical statues and body parts – as the inventory says, '17 hands and arms, cast from life'.

Rembrandt painted here while his pupils made his paints and prepared the canvases.

Pigment and palette
The pigments were ground with linseed oil on a large, flat, hard stone – the grindstone – to make the paint.

The 17th-century artist had access to a limited number of pigments. There was smalt, a violet blue, made from ground glass; azurite, a bluish green mineral pigment; white lead and chalk were

used to make white paint; many yellow and red ochres were also used, as were lacquers made from insects or plants. Paint was made by mixing a pigment with oil as a binder. There were various types of oils. Linseed oil was widely used; it dries quite quickly and has an attractive glow. It was made by crushing linseed. Painters stored their pigments and binders in bottles and earthenware jars. They usually made paint in small quantities, just enough for one day. They used a palette knife to put a blob of paint on the palette. The knife was also used to mix the paint on the palette. Rembrandt sometimes used his palette knife to put the paint on the canvas: the marks are clearly visible in the paint.

The carrier, the easel and the brush
Early in his career, Rembrandt painted on panels, but later on he switched almost exclusively to canvas. Panels were made of oak. Here in the studio a few stretched canvases are leant against the wall. It is likely that Rembrandt bought his canvases ready prepared – coated with a ground. The canvas was then stretched on a wooden frame with the aid of cords.

The canvas, stretched on the frame, stood on the easel. The easel was positioned so that the light fell full on the canvas: slightly angled so that Rembrandt's own shadow would not be cast across its surface.

On a small table stand the painter's tools, among them the brushes. A painter owned numerous brushes – fine for the precise work and larger for coarser painting. Brushes were made from the hair of various animals, including ermine, badgers, martens and pigs.

When a painting was finished, it was stretched again and then framed.

Rembrandt's studio with a model c. 1655, drawing, Ashmolean Museum, Oxford

Rembrandt draws his studio

When it came to restoring the studio, the information in the inventory was augmented by a drawing by Rembrandt. On the right sits a model, possibly Hendrickje Stoffels. Part of the easel can be seen on the left; on the right there is a glimpse of the mantelpiece and the stove. The drawing was followed closely in the restoration: with the three-legged stool by the table, the shelves on the wall to the right and the sheet over the window. Even the panes of the leaded lights have been restored on the basis of the drawing.

THE CABINET
(Kunstcaemer)

Rembrandt was a man of the world. He was not just any artist: he was a scholarly one who enjoyed social standing, as his exceptional collection of art and rare objects from all over the world proves. Here Rembrandt had the world within reach, everything from stuffed and mounted globefish to plaster casts of classical statues, from prints by Raphael to assegais from Africa. Rembrandt collected things not only because he found them interesting and beautiful, but also so that he could use them as props in his work. His pupils also put their master's superb collection of curiosa to good use.

Rembrandt was a passionate – indeed obsessive – collector. Had he

not built up his collection, he would have been able to pay off the loan on his house and he would probably not have gone bankrupt. But Rembrandt needed his collection: he wanted to surround himself with all these beautiful and fascinating things from all four corners of the earth at any price.

Collecting tradition
In the 17th century it became extremely fashionable among the prosperous Dutch bourgeoisie to set up a cabinet of art and rare objects. The flourishing trade with distant lands meant that all sorts of unfamiliar exotic objects could be imported.

Rembrandt's collection included

artificialia and *naturalia. Artificialia* are objects made by man, such as paintings, statues, medals, decorative art objects and ethnographic artefacts, prints and books. *Naturalia* are objects from the natural world: stuffed animals, dried plants, stones and shells.

Reconstruction

Extraordinary creatures hang from the ceiling and rare objects produced by man and nature are arranged along the shelves on the walls. Hundreds of objects together present a fascinating picture of Rembrandt as a collector, although they do not come from his collection. Rembrandt's collection was

sold and broken up when he went bankrupt in 1656. The objects that have now been brought together in the cabinet are similar to those in Rembrandt's collection. From the descriptions in the inventory we have a fairly accurate idea of the rarities and objets d'art in the collection. 'Two globes, a box of minerals, a pewter pot, a pissing child, two East Indian dishes, a bust of the Emperor Augustus, a Nero, two iron helmets ...' The objects have as far as possible been placed in the order of their listing in the inventory.

Using the art collection

Rembrandt and his pupils used the collection as study material and as a source of inspiration for their own work. As a history painter, Rembrandt painted exemplary stories from the Old and New Testaments, from classical mythology and from history. In dressing these scenes from the past, he used items from his art collection. Elements taken from prints by other artists, weapons, headdresses and other objects in the collection appear in Rembrandt's drawings and paintings.

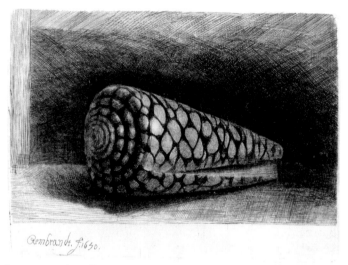

Rembrandt f.1650.

own work, among them the bust of Homer, which he used in his famous painting *Aristotle Contemplating the Bust of Homer,* dating from 1653.

Rembrandt owned around 8000 prints and drawings by illustrious contemporaries and predecessors like Michelangelo, Raphael, Titian, Rubens, Holbein, Dürer and Lucas van Leyden, which he kept in large folders and albums. These works of art were an important source of inspiration for Rembrandt's own work.

Rembrandt went on collecting
Rembrandt's property was sold at auction shortly after the inventory was taken. But this sale did not put paid to Rembrandt's collecting passion. In the course of 1658 the artist moved to a house he rented on the Rozengracht, where he again surrounded himself with art and valuable objects.

Conus Marmoreus
Many of the *naturalia* were displayed 'on the hindmost shelf' in the cabinet: 'a great quantity of horns, sea creatures . . ..' One of these sea creatures – a shell – was the subject of a still life etching. This shell, the *conus marmoreus* or marbled shell, was found in the Indian Ocean. Rembrandt studied the shell closely but was apparently not concerned that the printing process would reverse the image. The spiral now runs anti-clockwise, something that never happens in nature.

Statues and prints
Rembrandt had some sixty statues. Copies of classical busts were a prominent feature in his collection. Some of these heads appear in his

THE SMALL STUDIO
(Cleijne Schildercaemer)

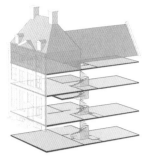

This attic room with the low beams was used by Rembrandt's pupils. Separate cubicles were created here with wooden partitions or curtains so that the pupils – four or five at a time – could work undisturbed.

Self-portrait drawing at a window 1648, etching

The Rembrandt House is Rembrandt's old home, but it is also the only place in the world where his graphic art is on permanent display and where exhibitions on this subject are regularly staged. Changing selections from Rembrandt's etched oeuvre are on show in the new wing.

Rembrandt was a multi-faceted artist: he was the most famous painter of his age, an extraordinarily gifted draughtsman *and* an unsurpassed etcher. His keen eye, virtuoso technique and individual approach imbued his etchings with a personal character.

He first started experimenting with graphic art around 1625/1626, when he had just established himself as an independent artist in Leiden. The first dated etchings were made in 1628.

Rembrandt continued to produce prints until about 1661. In this period, spanning more than 35 years, he made some 290 prints. He almost always pulled several impressions from one plate. These impressions were extremely popular with collectors and were very important in broadcasting Rembrandt's fame as an artist. In 1660 the famous Italian painter Guercino wrote to the Sicilian aristocrat and connoisseur Don Antonio Ruffo, 'I have seen various of his printed works which have reached this country; they are very finely executed, sensitively and skilfully etched ... And I regard him unequivocally as a great virtuoso'.

Rembrandt's etching style was exceptional. He explored the possibilities of the technique more intensely than any other artist.

Many of his prints exist in several versions, known as 'states' – sometimes more than ten. Rembrandt experimented with the etching technique by making different impressions, adding something, or taking something away. This approach also meant that he satisfied the acquisitiveness of collectors. Some of them wanted to own all the etchings by the master: the different states of the same work sold like hot cakes.

Rembrandt's etchings are built up of spontaneous, sketch-like lines. The definition of light and dark passages is achieved by allowing some lines to be bitten out more deeply than others. Subtle hatching creates dramatic lighting effects. In 1686 Rembrandt's technique was praised by the Florentine artist Filippo Baldinucci, who wrote of 'Rembrandt's extraordinary manner of etching ... which is characterized by the free and irregular use of line, without delineation of outlines, and which results in a deep, powerful chiaroscuro of painterly quality'.

One way that Rembrandt achieved this painterly effect was by combining the technique of etching with the use of drypoint. From about 1640 onwards, the artist made increasing use of the drypoint technique, which can be recognized by the velvety lines it produces. He actually made some prints entirely by this technique, working directly into the copper plate without an etching ground – the first artist ever to do so.

Self-portraits

Whereas in his paintings Rembrandt concentrated chiefly on depicting the subjects that enjoyed great prestige at the time – stories from the Bible and from history – in his prints he explored a much broader range of subjects and themes. He etched biblical scenes, landscapes, nudes, beggars, portraits, allegories, a still life and several book illustrations.

Among Rembrandt's earliest prints is a small group of etchings in which he portrayed his own face, each time with a different expression – laughing, pensive, looking anxious or angry. The Rembrandt in this little etching is not yet 25. He looks up in surprise, with raised eyebrows and pursed lips. It is a very small print and the framing of the face is tight: part of Rembrandt's cap is out of the picture.

In his early years Rembrandt often used his own face as an object of study. He tried out all sorts of effects – expressions, emotions – in the mirror, and he also used his own head to study the working of light and shade.

This Rembrandt self-portrait is a prime example of the skill with which he was able to capture facial expressions, in this case extreme surprise.

Self-portrait looking amazed 1630, etching

Self-portrait 1630, etching

Rembrandt made this self-portrait
in 1630. The artist glares at the viewer from under a bush of wildly curl-
ing hair.

Self-portrait leaning on a wall 1639, etching

He also used his own face to portray himself as a gentleman of standing. In this print, a self-assured Rembrandt looks out at the viewer. He borrowed the striking pose – arm resting on the balustrade – from a portrait by Titian. Perhaps he wanted to compete with his illustrious predecessor and this is why he chose to model himself on such a famous work. Borrowings of this kind were not unusual among artists.

Rembrandt's mother in a headscarf 1633, etching

Tronies

Rembrandt made studies of his own face, and he also recorded other striking heads. These studies of male and female heads are known as 'tronies'. They were not intended as portraits; he used them as he did his self-portraits as studies in the rendition of light and shade, and different expressions. Rembrandt made most of his tronies between 1630 and 1640. He was particularly fond of portraying old, wrinkled, lived-in faces.

Old man with a beard c. 1631, etching

Saskia wearing pearls in her hair 1634, etching

Portraits

The distinction between a tronie
and a portrait is not always clear,
although essentially a tronie is concerned with a typical head whereas
a portrait is primarily about captur-
ing a likeness. Rembrandt etched
some twenty portraits. It seems
likely that they were originally
intended for private use rather than
for sale. Many of the sitters were
friends or relatives of Rembrandt's.

The early portraits are simple in
conception and technique. The later
ones, like that of Jan Six, which
dates from 1647, are much more
detailed, and executed with considerable thought about the effect of
the light.

Leaning nonchalantly on the
windowsill, Jan Six reads a book in
the light that enters through the
window behind him. The heavy
curtain surrounds the window
frame and Six. The books and man-
uscripts on the chair in the foreground and the painting on the wall
illustrate his erudition and his love
of art. The work is technically
extremely accomplished and has
always been one of Rembrandt's
most admired prints. Rembrandt
drew an infinite number of tiny
lines with an etching needle and
drypoint to achieve this painterly
effect.

Jan Six 1647, etching

Everyday life

Rembrandt was also fascinated by scenes of everyday life, as we can see from his etching of a group of beggars standing at a door. The impoverished family is portrayed down to the smallest detail – the man, the woman with the baby strapped on her back, and the little boy. The scene centres on the two hands as the householder drops alms into the woman's outstretched palm.

Rembrandt left the right-hand side of the plate blank. Contemporaries commented on these unworked areas, complaining that they made his prints appear 'unfinished', but Rembrandt was indifferent to this criticism. According to the artist's biographer Arnold Houbraken, Rembrandt believed that 'a piece is finished when the master has achieved what he set out to do'.

Family of beggars at the door of a house 1648, etching

Man making water 1631, etching

Woman making water 1631, etching

In 1631 Rembrandt made two small etchings that belong together – of a man and a woman passing water. Seldom has this most mundane of everyday activities been rendered so frankly.

Landscapes

Most of Rembrandt's landscape etchings were made in the years between 1640 and 1653. At this time he was living in his house in the Breestraat and often went for walks outside the city, taking the road to Diemen or beside the River Amstel to Ouderkerk. He made innumerable sketches of what he saw on the

The three trees 1643, etching

way. Later, in his studio, he worked these drawings up into etchings.

The Three Trees is one of Rembrandt's most famous landscape prints. The trees were on the Diemerzeedijk: the Amsterdam skyline can be seen in the background. The threatening sky and the false sunlight create a dramatic effect.

The 'Omval' 1645, etching

This bend in the Amstel is still known as the Omval. There is a fine contrast between the detailed rendition of the moss-grown pollarded willow in the foreground – in which we can discern a pair of lovers – and the telling, swiftly drawn prospect on the right, with boats, houses and a windmill. Rembrandt made extensive use of the drypoint technique in this etching; it is particularly noticeable in the tree.

Jupiter and Antiope 1659, etching

Nudes

Antiope, the daughter of the King of Thebes, lies sleeping, naked, on a great pile of cushions, totally relaxed, her mouth slightly open. She is completely unaware that she is being ogled by the Greek god Jupiter, who has disguised himself as a satyr. Rembrandt chose this mythological story as the subject of a mildly erotic print. His etching technique here is matchless: dark, velvety hatching for the shadows interspersed with light, barely-worked passages.

Naked woman sitting on a mound c. 1631, etching

Rembrandt portrayed this woman uncompromisingly nude, entirely at odds with the prevailing ideal of beauty. Rembrandt depicted her body exactly as he saw it in front of him, with sagging belly, slack breasts, fat thighs and bony knees. In 1681 Rembrandt was described as 'the first heretic in art', because, wrote Andries Pels:

'Were he to paint a naked woman, as he sometimes did,
No Grecian Venus did he as model bid,
But a washerwoman, or a peat stamper from a shed,
Calling his deviance following where Nature led,
And all the rest vain ornament. Slack breasts,
Twisted hands, even the marks of the laces
Of the corset on the belly, the garters 'round the legs,
All must be followed or Nature was not content.'

Biblical scenes

The Old and New Testaments feature prominently in Rembrandt's oeuvre. While Rembrandt based his work on the text of the Bible, he certainly also drew on the pictorial tradition. We can often identify motifs in the prints that have been borrowed from the work of his predecessors. Many of the prints that served Rembrandt as models were in his own collection.

This print of Adam and Eve, for example, is derived from a work by Albrecht Dürer dating from 1504. Eve is on the point of giving Adam the forbidden fruit, the apple of the tree of knowledge of good and evil. The devil himself is present in the shape of a monster with claws. The trumpeting elephant in the background – a reference to the time when man and the animals lived together in peace – is an altogether jollier creature.

The Fall of Man 1638, etching

The Bible tells us that, as Christ was being crucified, darkness fell over the whole earth in the middle of the day. Rembrandt captured the drama of this event in his largest print *The Three Crosses*. A strong shaft of light cleaves the darkness and illuminates the crucified Christ in the centre. Jesus himself, raised above the tumult, radiates a serene peace.

In making this print, Rembrandt

The three crosses 1653, dry-point

abandoned the etching technique and drew straight into the copper with drypoint and burin. Years after he made the first impressions, he reworked the plate, changing the whole scene. Rembrandt constantly revisited his work – always improving on himself, always seeking the best solution.

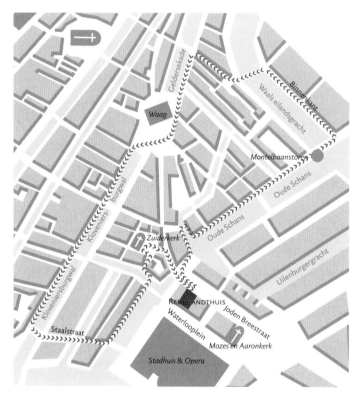

The Montelbaanstoren c. 1645, drawing, The Rembrandt House Museum

This area was originally known as the Lastage, the site of boat sheds and rope walks. This is where ships were repaired, provisioned for their voyage and loaded with ballast.

Rembrandt drew the Montelbaanstoren from a bridge that no longer exists. The tower was built in 1516 to defend the Lastage, which was outside the dykes. The tower lost its function when the defences were modernized and extended after 1578. New fortifications were built and the height of the Montelbaanstoren was reduced – probably at the same time. In 1606 a clock tower was built on the base of the tower. The octagonal superstructure with the decorative spire was designed by the city architect Hendrick de Keyser. The work was prompted by local residents, who complained that they could not hear any clock chimes and so never knew what time it was. A tall spire also created a landmark in the city.

The walk starts outside The Rembrandt House, Jodenbreestraat 4.

Standing on the steps outside the Rembrandt House, look diagonally left and you will see the Sint Anthoniessluis (a canal lock).

Cross over the road to the left, towards the lock. Walk along the Oude Schans, heading towards the Montelbaanstoren.

Rembrandt drew the tower without its spire, even though it was certainly there when he made the drawing. Rembrandt may have wanted to show only the original medieval part, without later additions, although he did draw the harbour master's house, built on piles, at the foot of the tower.

Cross the bridge by the Montel-baanstoren, turn left into the Binnenkant. Continue as far as the bridge on the left. Cross the bridge, turn right into the Binnen Bantammerstraat. At the end of the street turn left into the Geldersekade.

Abraham Wilmerdonckx, merchant and governor of the Dutch West India Company, lived at number 119 Geldersekade. He commissioned Rembrandt to paint a portrait of himself and his wife around 1640. This double portrait has not survived.

Walk on to the Nieuwmarkt

The building in the centre of the square is De Waag (the weigh-house). It was originally the Sint Anthoniespoort, the eastern city gate, built in 1488. When the city was extended in 1585 the city wall was built beyond the gate, leaving it inside the city and redundant as a gateway. In 1617 it was converted into a weigh-house.

The surgeon's guild met in this building. The famous physician, Professor Nicolaes Tulp, was the praelector (lecturer) of this guild and it was he who commissioned Rembrandt to paint a portrait of the surgeons in 1632. *The Anatomy Lesson of Dr Nicolaes Tulp* was Rembrandt's first group portrait. It was a prestigious commission for the 26-year-old painter, who had only recently come to live in Amsterdam. The painting hung in De Waag until

the nineteenth century. It is now in the Mauritshuis in The Hague.

Cross the Nieuwmarkt and follow the route along the even-num-bered side of the Kloveniersburg-wal.

The majestic building across the canal is the Trippenhuis. It was built by Justus Vingboons in 1642 for the Trip brothers. They were dealers in cannons, arms and munitions. Rembrandt painted portraits of their parents, Jacob Trip and Margaretha de Geer.

In the nineteenth century, the forerunner of the Rijksmuseum was housed in this building and Rembrandt's *The Night Watch* hung here. The painting was moved to the new Rijksmuseum building with the rest of the collection in 1884.

Continue along the Kloveniers-burgwal to the lift bridge on the left.

The spot where the Doelenhotel now stands was once the site of the militia rifle range – the 'doelen'. This was where the militia met. Militiamen were citizens who were given the task of maintaining public order. The Amsterdam Kloveniers, whose headquarters stood on this site, commissioned a group portrait from Rembrandt to decorate their Great Hall. This portrait was Rembrandt's world-famous *The Night Watch*; the painting hung here.

Go back through the Staalstraat.

The Staalstraat was the centre of the Amsterdam cloth industry. The building that is now number 7a-b was part of the Staalhof, a large complex for cloth manufacturing. Rembrandt's last large group portrait, *The Syndics of the Cloth Makers' Guild,* hung in one of the rooms in the Staalhof. It is a portrait of the

men who checked the quality of the cloth. This painting, which also hung in the Trippenhuis, is now in the Rijksmuseum.

Continue along the Staalstraat, cross the bridge and, before you reach the second bridge, turn left into the Zwanenburgwal. Go straight on, cross the bridge, and then immediately turn left. Take the first turning on the right to the Zuiderkerk.

Rembrandt also drew the Zuiderkerk. Here again he left the spire off, just as he did when he drew the Montelbaanstoren. This church, designed by Hendrick de Keyser, was the first Protestant church to be built in Amsterdam.

The first three children born to Rembrandt and his wife Saskia were buried in this church. Titus was baptized here on 22 September 1641.

Rembrandt must often have heard the bells of the Zuiderkerk.

Go back along the Anthonies-breestraat to the Jodenbreestraat and the Rembrandt House.

Author:
  Fieke Tissink
Translation:
  Lynne Richards
Photographs:
  Sjaak Henselmans
Groundplan:
  Paul Maas and
  Eric van Rootselaar
Design:
  Antoon De Vylder, Herentals (B)
Typesetting:
  De Diamant Pers, Herentals (B)
Printing:
  Die Keure, Brugge (B)

ISBN 90 76588 30 9
NUR 643, 420

First edition, 2003;
second edition, 2005.